SNACKS & APPETIZERS

Uhrichsville, Ohio

Published by Barbour Publishing, Inc.
              P.O. Box 719
              Uhrichsville, Ohio 44683
              http://www.barbourbooks.com

Member of the
Evangelical Christian
Publishers Association

Printed in the United States of America.

LOLLIPOPS

1 loaf bread dough
(make into little balls)
Cook together:
1 cup brown sugar
2 cups water
3 T. butter

Pour over bread and bake at 350°F for about
30 minutes. Delicious with ice cream.

Julianne Troyer—Conneautville, PA

POPCORN BALLS

1 cup unpopped popcorn
1 tsp. salt
1/2 cup butter
1 lb. marshmallows
1/2 tsp. vanilla

Pop the popcorn, then salt it. Pour into a 9x13-inch pan. Melt butter and marshmallows in the top of a double boiler. Remove from heat, add vanilla, and food coloring of choice. Pour over popcorn; mix well. Butter hands, and quickly form into balls. Wrap each "ball" in a plastic wrap.

Jackie Jeffries—Pottstown, PA

PARTY MUSHROOMS

30 large, fresh mushrooms
6 oz. cream cheese
1/2 pkg. dry Ranch Dressing mix

Remove stems from mushrooms. Put stems and caps in boiling water for 1 minute. Drain. Cut up stems in fine, diced pieces. Mix stems, cream cheese, and Ranch Dressing. Spoon into caps. Microwave until warm.

Nancy Schwartz—Normal, IL

BEEFY CHEESE BALL

3 8-oz. cream cheese (room temp.)
1 small can mushrooms, chopped
1 small can black olives, chopped
1 small jar dried beef, chopped
2 T. of accent
1 small bunch of green onions, chopped
    (green stems only)

Mix all ingredients together, shape into balls and refrigerate. May decorate with paprika. Serve with crackers. (Can freeze; can also serve as a dip.)

Linda McKinney—Pontotoc, MS

CARAMEL CORN

8 cups popped popcorn
    (about 1/3 cup unpopped)
3/4 cup packed brown sugar
6 T. margarine
3 T. light corn syrup

Spread popcorn out on a 17x12x2-inch baking pan; set aside. For caramel mixture, in a heavy sauce-pan combine the brown sugar, margarine, and corn syrup. Cook and stir over medium heat until mixture starts to boil. Continue cooking 5 more minutes and remove from heat. Pour over popcorn and place in a 300ºF oven for 10 minutes. Remove and stir. Replace for 5 more minutes. Remove again and stir. Replace for 5 more minutes and remove one last time. Turn the caramel popcorn out onto foil. Cool; break into 1-inch pieces and store in air-tight container.

Bonnie Wentz—Woodbury, PA

NAVAJO FRY BREAD

2 cups flour
1/2 cup dry milk
3 tsp. baking powder
1/2 tsp. salt

2 T. shortening
1/2 cup water
4 T. oil
Various toppings: Margarine, honey, maple syrup, cinnamon sugar

Sift first four ingredients. Add the shortening and with your fingertips, rub the flour and shortening together until it has a flaky consistency. Pour in the water and toss until the dough can be gathered into a ball. Cover with a towel and let it rest 20 minutes. Cut into three pieces. Roll out into 8-inch circles, 1/4-inch thick. Cut two 4 or 5-inch parallel slits completely through the dough. In a 10-inch skillet, heat oil. Fry one at a time for 2 minutes, each side. Serve warm with margarine, honey, maple syrup, or cinnamon sugar.

Monya Riera—Summerville, SC

FRUIT PIZZA

CRUST

1/2 cup butter or margarine
1/4 cup brown sugar
1 egg
1 1/3 cups flour
1 tsp. baking powder
1/4 tsp. salt

Cream together butter, sugar, and egg. Add baking powder and 1/4 tsp. salt. Press in greased pizza pan and bake 10 minutes at 375ºF.

FILLING

8 oz. cream cheese
1/2 cup powdered sugar
8 or 10 oz. whipped topping

Cream together and spread on cooled crust. On top of this arrange in circles sliced fresh fruit, such as apples, grapes, oranges, kiwis, strawberries, pineapples, etc.

2 cups pineapple juice
1/2 cup sugar
1 T. gelatin
2 T. orange gelatin

Cook until clear. Cool and spread over the fruit.

Barbara Graber—Quincy, MI

BARBECUPS
Yield: 20 barbecups

3/4 lb. ground beef
1/2 cup barbecue sauce
2 T. brown sugar
1 can of 10 buttermilk biscuits
3/4 cup shredded cheese
1 T. minced onion

Preheat oven to 400ºF. In a large skillet, brown the meat and drain. Add barbecue sauce, onion, and brown sugar. Simmer for 5 minutes. Separate biscuits into halves and press and mold into a greased muffin pan. Spoon the mixture into muffin cups. Top with the shredded cheese. Bake at 400°F for about 12 minutes or until golden brown. Remove gently with spoon after allowing to cool.

Pamela Bass—Elberton, GA

RYE BOAT

1 pt. sour cream
1 1/3 cups mayonnaise
1 small onion, grated
1 small jar chipped (dried) beef, chopped
Rye bread

Mix all ingredients. Serve with rye bread or pumpernickel bread chunks. Or hollow out 1 round loaf rye bread; fill with dip, arrange cubed bread (from what was hollowed out around shell).

Audrey J. Wall—Industry, PA

SAUSAGE CHEESE BALLS
Yield: 75 small balls

3 cups biscuit mix
8 oz. grated cheddar cheese
1 lb. raw mild sausage (room temp.)

Mix thoroughly with hands until you can't distinguish cheese, from sausage, from biscuit mix. Roll into small balls, about bite-sized. Bake on cookie sheet at 350°F for about 15 minutes or until golden brown. They can be made ahead of time and warmed up later.

Ora McClellan—Bowie, MD

LITTLE PIZZAS

1 lb. ground beef
1 lb. cheese
1 lb. hot sausage
1/2 tsp. each:

oregano, garlic powder, onion powder, salt
English muffins

Brown beef and sausage in skillet. Drain fat. Add cut-up cheese, and all of the spices. Simmer over low-heat and spread on halved English muffins. Broil 4-5 minutes.

Ora McClellan—Bowie, MD

CHRISTMAS BREAKFAST PIZZA

1 lb. pork sausage
1 1/2 cups milk
1 lb. processed cheese, chunked
6 slices loaf bread
10 eggs
8 oz. mozzarella cheese

Seasoning:
Creole seasoning
1/4 cup onion, chopped
1/4 cup black olives, chopped

Italian seasoning
1/4 cup bell peppers, chopped
1/4 cup mushrooms, chopped

Brown sausage; drain. In 9x13-inch pan or 2 smaller casseroles, grease and crumble bread to form first layer. Crumble sausage over this. In separate bowl, mix seasoning ingredients together. Pour this over sausage. Layer cheeses over this. In separate bowl, beat eggs and stir in milk. Pour this over the layers. DO NOT STIR! Cover and place in refrigerator overnight. Remove cover and bake at 325ºF for approximately 20 minutes. Do not overbake. Remove when cheese is melted. Serve with biscuits and tomatoes.

Karen Carroll—Smithville, MS

POPOVER PIZZA

1 lb. of hamburger or sausage
1 large chopped onion
15 oz. pizza sauce
4 oz. sliced mushrooms
8 oz. shredded mozzarella
Various pizza fixings
1/2 cup parmesan cheese
2 eggs
1 cup milk
1 T. oil
1 cup flour
1/2 tsp. salt

Brown the meat and onion; drain. Stir in the pizza sauce. Pour into greased 9x13-inch pan. Top with mushrooms and other pizza fixings (pepperoni, green peppers or whatever you like); top with mozzarella cheese. Beat eggs, milk, and oil until foamy. Add flour and salt, beat until smooth. Pour over meat mixture, spread to cover. Sprinkle with parmesan cheese. Bake at 400°F for 30 minutes. It can be doubled and will still fit in 9x13-inch pan. Just bake a little longer.

Deb Brown—Coldwater, MI

OVER-NIGHT COFFEE CAKE
Yield: 15 servings

3/4 cup margarine, softened
1 cup sugar
Combine and cream until light and fluffy.

Add:
2 eggs, beaten
1 cup sour cream
Mix well.

Add:
2 cups flour
1 tsp. soda
1 tsp. baking powder.
Combine well. Pour batter into greased, floured 9x13-inch pan.

Combine:
3/4 cup brown sugar, firmly packed
1/2 cup chopped nuts
1 tsp. cinnamon

Mix well and sprinkle over batter. Cover and refrigerate overnight. Uncover and bake at 350°F for 35 or 40 minutes or until cake tests done.

Charlotte Pardoe—Glen Burnie, MD

VEGETABLE TREE

2 tubes crescent rolls
Cream cheese spread
Broccoli
Cauliflower
Cherry tomatoes

Shape dough into a tree on a cookie sheet. Bake at 375°F for 8 minutes or until golden brown. Cool. Prepare cream cheese spread (see next recipe) and cover crust. Press small sprigs of broccoli into cheese spread. Decorate with "garland" of tiny sprigs of cauliflower. Accent with small cherry tomatoes (halved). Refrigerate several hours before serving.

CREAM CHEESE SPREAD & DIP

16 oz. cream cheese, room temperature
1 small onion
1 clove garlic
1/4 tsp. horseradish
Milk to make right consistency

Blend all ingredients in blender, adding milk as needed. Adjust onion, garlic, and horse-radish to taste. Add food coloring if desired.

Arlene Knickerbocker—Davison, MI

GUACAMOLE
Yield: 1.5 cups

2 soft, pitted, peeled avocados
1 T. grated onion or dried onion
1 T. lemon juice
1 tsp. salt
1/2 tsp. chili powder
1/3 cup mayonnaise

Mash avocados with fork. Stir in onion, lemon juice, salt, and chili powder. Spread mayonnaise over mixture, sealing to edges of bowl; chill. At serving time, blend mayonnaise into mixture. Serve with corn or flour tortilla chips, and crackers.

Veronica Arnold—Ft. Collins, CO

FRENCH DIP SANDWICHES

Thin slices of French bread
Butter
Beef broth
Leftover roast beef, thinly sliced
Grated mozzarella cheese

Spread slices of bread with butter. Toast buttered side up under oven broiler until golden brown. Place roast beef slices and grated cheese on half of the bread on unbuttered side. Top each slice with another slice of bread. Heat in microwave or conventional oven until cheese melts. Serve with a cup of beef broth from leftover pot roast. Or dissolve beef bouillon cubes in boiling water. Add chopped green peppers, onions, and dill weed. Simmer 15 minutes before serving.

Veronica Arnold—Ft. Collins, CO

HOLIDAY MEATBALLS

1 1/2 lb. ground beef
3/4 cup bread crumbs
1 egg
2 T. water
2 tsp. sugar
1 small onion, minced
1 tsp. salt
1/2 tsp. pepper
Cooking oil
1/2 cup grape jelly
1/2 cup hamburger relish

Mix all ingredients together in mixing bowl, except jelly and relish. Form into small meatballs. Brown meatballs in frying pan with small amount of cooking oil. Then glaze with jelly and relish. Let simmer 30 minutes with a lid on it. Stir 2-3 times so meatballs are well coated with sauce. Serve hot.

Luella Nelsen—Jamestown, NY

MEXICAN CHICKEN

2 lb. boneless chicken breasts, chopped in
    cubes and cooked
Garlic salt
Pepper
1 large onion, diced
1 lb. processed cheese, cubed
1 12-oz. can tomatoes with chilies
1 medium bag of nacho flavor corn chips,
    crushed
2 cans cream of chicken soup
Additional corn chips
Sour cream

Preheat oven to 400°F. Sprinkle chicken
with garlic salt and pepper to taste. In a
large mixing bowl, add all ingredients
together. Pour into a well-greased casserole or baking dish. Bake at 400°F for 45
minutes, until cheese and sauce bubbles.
Serve hot with sour cream and extra chips.

Thom Britton—Three Rivers, MI

CRABMEAT SNACKS

1 can crabmeat
1/2 cup margarine
2 jars old english cheese
English muffins

Mix first three ingredients. Spread on toasted English muffin halves. Just before serving broil until bubbly, about 5 minutes.

Arlene Knickerbocker—Davison, MI

JANE'S PUNCH
Yield: 16 servings

1 32-oz. bottle cranberry juice
10 cups water
2 cups sugar
1/4 cup lemon juice
2 cups orange juice
4 sticks cinnamon
1 tsp. whole cloves

Mix all ingredients and heat through. Simmer for 20-30 minutes. Serve hot. This punch is reheatable.

Mrs. Charles Sharp—Danville, KY

CRAB RANGOONS

8 oz. crabmeat
8 oz. cream cheese, softened
1/2 tsp. steak sauce
Garlic powder
Wonton wrappers

Mix meat, cheese, sauce, and powder together to paste consistency. Place a heaping teaspoon of mixture in center of each wonton wrapper. Gather the corners together and moisten with beaten egg white. Twist to seal. Deep fry 3 minutes and serve hot with favorite dips. Suggested sauces: BBQ, honey mustard, sweet and sour, blue cheese, ranch.

Saria Bushmire—Connellsville, PA

DILL DIP FOR VEGGIES

1 cup mayonnaise
1 cup sour cream
1 tsp. seasoned salt
1 T. chopped parsley
1 T. dillweed
1 T. dry onion flakes
Dab of lemon juice

Mix well. Serve.

Rosanna Walter—Odessa, WA

FRUIT DIP

8 oz. softened cream cheese
1/2 cup brown sugar
1/2 tsp. vanilla
Fresh fruit

Blend cream cheese until smooth.
Then add the other ingredients. Serve with
fresh fruits.

Pamela S Vandevoort—Pella, IA

HOT MEXICAN SPINACH DIP

2 T. vegetable oil
1 medium onion, chopped
2 tomatoes, chopped
2 T. canned jalapenos, chopped
1 10-oz. package frozen spinach,
    chopped, thawed, and squeezed
1 T. red wine vinegar
2 cups monterey jack cheese, shredded
8 oz. cream cheese, cubed
1 cup half-and-half
5 oz. sliced black olives

Preheat oven to 400ºF. Heat oil in skillet over medium heat. Add onions and sauté until soft—about 4 minutes. Add tomatoes and jalapenos and cook another 2 minutes. Transfer to large bowl and stir in spinach, monterey jack cheese, cream cheese, half-and-half, olives, and vinegar. Season with salt and pepper. Spoon mixture into shallow oven-proof baking dish. Bake until bubbly and top is browned, about 35 minutes. Serve with tortilla chips.

Charlotte Shopmeyer—Evansville, IN

TACO DIP

1 can refried beans
16 oz. sour cream
8 oz. or less of salsa
1/2 cup red onion, chopped
Chopped chilis, optional
8 oz. cheddar cheese
7 oz. mozzarella cheese
Sliced black olives

Layer 9x13-inch glass dish with ingredients in order as listed. Chill.

Ora McClellan—Bowie, MD

CHRISTMAS BEEF BARBECUE

1 3-lb. roast beef, baked tender
16 oz. bottle of ketchup
1 tsp. horseradish sauce
2 shakes Tabasco sauce

After beef roast has cooled, shred apart in a large bowl. In a small bowl, mix ketchup, horseradish, and Tabasco sauce. Combine mixture with meat and cover until ready to use. When ready, warm mixture and serve on buns.

Margaret Layton Hunt—
Charlotte, North Carolina.

SUPER PARTY PUNCH
Yield: 30 servings

Bring to a boil 24 hours before serving time:

2 cups water
4 T. black tea (can use 4 tea bags)
2 cups sugar

Add 2 lemons (squeezed) and their juice to other ingredients and let steep for 10 minutes after it comes to a boil. Strain and cool.

4 cups cold water
1 tsp. vanilla
1 tsp. almond extract
Add these ingredients to the above mixture; let sit for 24 hours.

2 28-oz. bottles ginger ale
When ready to serve, add the ginger ale and ice—delicious!

Marge Cox—Topeka, KS

WASSAIL PUNCH

1 gallon apple cider
4 cups cranberry juice
6 sticks cinnamon
2-3 whole cloves, in teaball or cheesecloth
2 sweet oranges, sliced crosswise
1/2 cup brown sugar, optional

Mix all ingredients together in a large pot, and cook 1 hour on high (or 4 hours on low in crock pot). Remove orange slices and spices. Serve hot. This is reheatable.

Barbara Dyess—Colorado Springs, CO

ORANGE JULIUS

16 oz. can orange juice concentrate
1 cup milk
1 cup water
1/2 cup sugar

1 tsp. vanilla
1 tray ice cubes

Combine all ingredients in the blender and run until smooth.

Jenny Resendez—Port Arthur, TX

CHIMALE DIP

15 oz. can tamales
15 oz. can chili
1/4 cup picante sauce
8 oz. processed cheese spread, cubed
1/4 cup grated cheddar or
    Monterey Jack cheese

Drain liquid from tamales. Remove tamales from can and wrappers and mash with fork. Combine mashed tamales with chili, add the picante sauce and cubes of cheese. Place in 1 1/2 qt. casserole dish. Cover and heat in 350°F oven until hot and bubbly, about 20-

25 minutes. Sprinkle with grated cheese.
Serve hot with corn chips for dipping.

Veronica Arnold—Ft. Collins, CO

GRANDMA'S SURPRISE SALAD

2 pkg. red gelatin, any flavor
2 pkg. green gelatin, any flavor
1 container of whipped topping
1 14-oz. can of pineapple,
    crushed and drained
1 cup coconut, shredded
1/2 cup walnuts or pecans
Water

Following the package instructions, make
both packages of the green gelatin. Pour it
into a jelly roll pan or a cookie sheet with
sides. Refrigerate 1 1/2 hours or longer. Cut
the green gelatin into cubes and set aside. In
a large bowl, prepare the red gelatin accord-
ing to package instructions and mix in the

whipped topping a little at a time. Whisk or whip it until the topping dissolves. Next, fold in the drained pineapple, coconut, nuts, and green gelatin cubes. Pour into a gelatin mold or a large glass dish. Refrigerate overnight.

Julie Dutro—Hammond, IN

CADA FIESTA WORLD SERIES DIP

16 oz. can refried beans
4 oz. can diced green chilis
16 oz. sour cream
   (mix with taco seasoning)
1 pkg. taco seasoning mix
1 chopped tomato
1/2 cup chopped green or red onions
1 cup guacamole dip
4 oz. can black olives, chopped
1 cup cheddar cheese, grated

In shallow 12-inch bowl or plate, layer series of ingredients in order listed. Place container of dip on large platter and surround with tortilla chips.

Veronica Arnold—Ft. Collins, CO

FRUIT SOUP
Yield: 10-1 cup servings

1 package mixed dried fruits
1 12-oz. bag dried apricots
1/2 lemon—thinly sliced
2 T. quick-cooking tapioca
    (start with 2 and add, perhaps up to
    7 T. tapioca)
1/2 tsp. salt
1 cup granulated sugar
3 cinnamon sticks

Combine mixed dried fruits, apricots, lemon slices and 2 quarts water. Stir in tapioca, salt, sugar, and cinnamon sticks. Bring to a boil uncovered. Cover, and simmer over low heat—20-25 minutes or until fruits are fork-tender. Serve hot or cold.

Helen Smithlin—Sioux Falls, SD

CHICKEN SOUP

1 large chicken, cut up
1 medium onion, chopped
1 stalk celery, chopped
1 medium carrot, diced
3 chicken bouillon cubes
1 T. curry powder
2 tsp. poultry seasoning
Salt and pepper, optional
1/2 small pkg. tiny abc noodles

Boil chicken in water and cover until tender. Remove meat from bones and cut in pieces. Refrigerate overnight or several hours. Cool boiling liquid in large bowl overnight. When cold, chicken fat will rise to top. Skim off fat. Bring liquid back to boil. Add onion, celery, and carrot. Cook about 30 minutes. Add curry powder, poultry seasoning, and chicken cubes. Add salt and pepper if desired. Add noodles and cook until noodles are done.

Lorraine Pierce—Cut Off, LA

TACO SOUP

1 1/2 quarts tomato juice
1/4 cup sugar
1 pint corn
15 oz. kidney beans
1 lb. hamburger, browned
2 T. dried onion

Mix together in saucepan; simmer 5 minutes.

24 oz. bag tortilla chips
8 oz. sour cream
16 oz. shredded cheese

Serve soup over crushed chips. Top with sour cream and sprinkle with cheese.

Kary Martin—Myerstown, PA

TENNESSEE CAVIAR
Yield: 30 servings

3 cans black-eyed peas
1 can whole hominy
1 1/2 cups onion, diced
2 medium tomatoes, chopped
1 cup green onion, chopped
2 cups green peppers, diced
1 4-oz. can green chilies, chopped
1 2-oz. jar pimento
1 T. garlic, minced
1/2 cup fresh parsley, chopped
1 16-oz. bottle Italian dressing
Salt and pepper, to taste

Drain everything that is in cans and jars. Mix all ingredients in a large bowl. Refrigerate at least 6 hours. Remove to serving bowl with slotted spoon and serve with corn chips.

Terry Nielsen—Half Moon Bay, CA

CANADIAN CHEDDAR SOUP
Yield: 4 servings

2 cups water
1 lb. sharp cheddar cheese, grated
2 T. corn starch
2 cups evaporated milk
1 cup chopped broccoli
1/2 cup chopped carrots
8 oz. sliced mushrooms
butter or margarine
1/2 lb. Canadian bacon, cubed
1 T. Worcestershire sauce

Sauté broccoli in butter; empty into dish. Repeat with carrots, then with mushrooms. Set aside. Bring water to rolling boil in large pan (4-5 quart pan); lightly mix grated cheese and cornstarch. Add cheese mixture, a little at a time, stirring constantly, to the boiling water. Keep at rolling boil. Continue until all cheese is used and melted completely. Add vegetables, Worchestershire sauce, Canadian bacon, and heat thoroughly on low temperature. Add canned milk (undiluted), warm up, then serve.

Glenda Detherow—Bowling Green, KY

HEARTY MINESTRONE SOUP

1/2 T. oil
1 medium onion
1/4 tsp. garlic
1 pkg. frozen Italian mixed vegetables
1 can chopped tomatoes
1 cup tomato juice
1 cup chicken broth
1 1/2 tsp. sugar
1 tsp. Italian seasoning
1 to 2 T. basil
1/8 tsp. pepper
1 can northern beans
1/2 can elbow macaroni
1/4 cup parmesan cheese

Sauté onions and garlic; add vegetables,

tomatoes, tomato juice, broth, basil, and pepper. Cover and bring to a boil. Reduce heat to low and add macaroni and beans. Cook for 20 minutes.

Kellee Lehman—Carrbero, NC

BUTTER GLACE SOUP

Leftover roast chicken
1/2 cup Cream of Wheat
1 egg, separated
1/2 tsp. ground allspice
1 T. butter
Salt (to taste)

Put the leftover chicken and bones in a large pot of water. Bring to a boil and add three whole cloves and one bay leaf. Turn heat to medium and cook gently for another 20 minutes. Allow to cool slightly so you can skim off fat, taking out cloves and bay leaf. Meanwhile, in small bowl, combine 1/2 cup Cream of Wheat, one egg yolk, a tablespoon of butter, pinch of salt and 1/2 teaspoon ground allspice. Mix together. This will be the "butter glace" (pronounced "booter glazse") dumplings, and it will be thick. In separate bowl, whip the egg white until it stands in peaks. Gently fold it into the butter glace mixture, until absorbed. Return chicken broth to stove, bringing to a boil. With a teaspoon, gently take out about 1/2 teaspoon measurement of the butter glace mixture, and with the tip of another teaspoon, slide the little dumpling off the first spoon into the boiling chicken broth. Work quickly so the first butter glaces won't get done before the last ones. Turn heat down to medium-high, just enough so there is still a slight boiling motion, and cook until butter glaces float to the top, about 10-15 minutes, depending on how big you made them. (If you have a really large pot, or are cooking for more than your family, make another recipe of the butter glace—it doesn't work to double it.)

Carol Schmidt—Stanwood, WA

CHEESE & POTATO WILD RICE SOUP

Yield: 8-10 servings

1/2 cup wild rice, uncooked
1 1/2 cups water
1/2 lb. bacon, cut in pieces
1/4 cup chopped onion
2 10 3/4-oz. cans of cream of potato soup
    (dilute with 1 cup liquid:
      1/2 milk, 1/2 water)
1 quart milk
2 1/2 cups grated American cheese

Combine rice and water in saucepan, cook over low heat for 45 minutes and drain; set aside. Fry bacon and onion until bacon is crisp—drain on paper towel. Place soup in large saucepan; dilute as directed. Stir in 1 quart of milk, bacon, onion, cheese and cooked rice.

Kelly Edwards—Dodge City, KS

NINE BEAN SOUP

2 cups bean soup mix
2 quarts water
1 lb. ham, diced
1 lg. onion, chopped
1/2 cup celery, chopped
1/2 cup carrot, chopped
1/2 tsp. basil
1/2 tsp. oregano
1/2 tsp. salt
1 bay leaf
1 16-oz. can stewed tomatoes

Soak beans overnight in water. Add all ingredients except tomatoes. Bring to boil, simmer 1 1/2 hours or until tender. Add tomatoes, simmer 30 minutes. In crockpot, cook on high 2 hours, then on low for 6 hours. Add tomatoes 1 hour before serving.

Note: Almost any combination of beans can be substituted for the Nine Bean Soup Mix.

Elaine Scheidler—Harrisburg, PA

POTATO SOUP

5 medium potatoes
2 stalks celery, chopped
2 medium carrots, diced
1 small onion, chopped
1 cup chicken broth
1 chicken bouillon cube
Salt to taste, pepper to taste
2 T. flour
2 cups milk
3 T. butter

Combine potatoes, celery, carrots, onion, broth, bouillon, salt, pepper, and butter. Cook covered about 15 minutes or until tender. Combine flour with small amount of milk until dissolved. Add to potato mixture along with remaining milk. Cook over medium heat until mixture starts to boil. (Can also add 3/4 cup of mozzarella cheese to soup.)

Holly Anderson—Inverness, IL

QUICK CORN RELISH

1/2 cup sugar
1/2 T. cornstarch
1/4 cup cider vinegar
1/4 cup water
1/8 tsp. salt
1 1/2 tsp. mustard seeds
2 cups drained whole kernel corn
1/4 cup chopped green pepper
1/4 cup chopped pimento

In medium saucepan, combine sugar, cornstarch, vinegar, water, salt, and mustard seed. Cook over medium heat until thickened. Cool. Add the rest of the ingredients. Stir. Put in covered bowl and refrigerate several hours or overnight.

Judy Pierson—Aragon, GA

CHICKEN NUGGETS

4-5 boneless, skinless chicken breasts, cubed
3/4 cup bread crumbs
1/2 cup flour
1 tsp. salt
1 tsp. pepper
1 egg
2 T. water
Shortening for frying

Heat shortening in deep fryer. Fry chicken cubes for approximately 10 minutes. Remove from heat and place on plate lined with paper towel. Mix together all of the other ingredients in a bowl and set aside. In small bowl, mix the egg and water together. Dip the chicken into the egg mixture and then into the dry mixture. Place in the deep fryer again and fry until golden brown. Serve with dipping sauces, such as BBQ sauce and honey.

Pam Goudzwaard—Oak Forest, IL

BARBECUE SAUCE
Yield: about 1 quart

1 32-oz. jar catsup
1/2 cup brown sugar
3/4 cup white sugar
1/3 cup Worcestershire sauce
1 tsp. salt
1 T. minced onion
1 T. flour
3 T. vinegar

Mix altogether. Cook until mixture thickens. Stir occasionally. Good on any kind of meat; especially good on fried pork chops. Spread thickly on top, then broil until brown.

Erma L. Stone—Commerce, OK

PEGGY'S SWEET POTATO CASSEROLE

3 cups fresh, cooked, sweet potatoes
1 cup sugar
3 eggs
1/2 cup milk
Dash salt
1 tsp. vanilla
1/2 stick margarine

Peel sweet potatoes, cover with water and simmer until tender. Drain. Mix sugar, eggs, milk, salt, vanilla, and margarine until smooth. Add to sweet potatoes. Pour into a greased 2-quart casserole. Cover with the following topping and bake, uncovered at 350°F for 30 minutes.

TOPPING

1 cup brown sugar
1/2 stick margarine, softened
1/4 cup flour
3/4 to 1 cup chopped pecans

Mix sugar, flour and softened margarine. Add pecans. Spread over top of sweet potatoes.

Betsy Batchelor—Raleigh, NC

DILL OYSTER CRACKERS

24 oz. oyster crackers
1 pkg. buttermilk ranch dressing mix
1 cup vegetable oil
1 tsp. dill weed
1/2 tsp. garlic powder or salt

Mix ingredients together except crackers. Pour mixture over the crackers. Stir until crackers are coated. Let stand 1 hour before serving.

Brenda Parrish—Gnadenhutten, OH